Kiddos & Mamas Do the Darndest Things

poems by

Sharon Waller Knutson

ISBN: 978-93-90601-94-3

First Edition: 2022
Rs. 200/-

Cyberwit.net
HIG 45 Kaushambi Kunj, Kalindipuram
Allahabad - 211011 (U.P.) India
http://www.cyberwit.net
Tel: +(91) 9415091004
E-mail: info@cyberwit.net

For Tammy and Becky and in memory of Heidi, whom I love as if they were my own children.

Acknowledgements

I'm grateful for these journals who published these poems in one form or another:

GAS Poetry, Art and Music: "Best Mom in the World."

Literary Mama: "His Mother" and "Lost."

ONE ART: "The Choice" and "Toads and Petroglyphs."

Orange Room Review: "Mistake."

Red Eft Review: "Roadie."

Rye Whiskey Review: "Barfly."

Sparks of Calliope: "Doppelganger Daughter."

The Drabble: "Suburban Stay at Home Mom."

The Five-Two: "Black Eyed Susan."

Verse-Virtual: "In Buddy's Bar and Grill," "Seven-Year-Old Twin Boys," and "The Woman With 15 Children."

Writing in a Woman's Voice: "In the Sixties Before Seat Belts and Dr. Phil."

Contents

The Kiddos

Nanny Love

I am still trying to figure out
how to get out of this nanny
gig and get myself into the dude
ranch kitchen so I can fall in love
with a real cowboy or handsome
stockbroker from Wall Street
vacationing in Wyoming when
a blonde toddler in a Winnie the Pooh
nightgown lying on her bed, blue eyes
staring through fringed blonde bangs.
picks me like a Pomeranian at the pound
names me Shanna and becomes my boss.

When she has a nightmare, she
calls out Shanna instead of Mommy
in her sleep and even if her mother
is standing right there, she wraps
her arms around my neck and her legs
around my waist and I carry her to my
bed and curl around her like a calico cat
until morning when she shakes me awake.

I am a bit worried she's getting too attached
to me and will be devastated when I leave
in the fall for college but her mother isn't.
You're not the first and you won't be the last.
She'll forget you the minute the new nanny
shows up. I'm more worried about you.
I am too because when my parents drive off

with me and the toddler runs after the car
shrieking *Shanna Come Back*, I sob as hard as her.

I figure she'd forget me in nine months.
But I am wrong. When I return
as a waitress at the dude ranch,
the next summer with my sister
as her new nanny, the almost three
year old is elated. *Shanna,*
it's about time you came back, she
sasses, taking my hand and pulling me
through the house to my room.

We decide not to tell her I am living
in a cabin just down the road. But we
underestimate the bloodhound and I soon
spot her standing on my doorstep
with her suitcase stuffed with gummy bears,
her jammies and *The Runaway Bunny.*
I'm living with you, she says firmly,
shrieking as my sister hauls her home.

When the dude ranch is full, the owner
rents my cabin to a socialite from So Ho
and pulls me out of the kitchen and puts
me up in his mansion on the hill to care
for his spoiled pampered princess
whose elderly nanny has flown off
to Berlin to tend to a family emergency.

The motherless girl, also a toddler, locks
herself in her room when I can't sing
the words to the German lullaby

her Kindermadchen had sung to her since she was
born. I miss Little Miss Sunshine and dread
morning when I'd have to braid the princess's
thick dark hair and make her Kaiserschmarrn
with lingonberry jam instead of cornflakes.

Just then my sister calls with news that my mini
me is missing. I suggest she try my old cabin.
Oh no, here she comes, stinking of Channel No 5
and covered in red lipstick and powder.
I hear a little voice*: Shanna wasn't home.*
My sister puts her on the phone. *Where are you?*
she demands as my other charge comes out
and crawls in my lap. *I'll be home, soon*, I say
and hang up the phone thinking this nanny business
is as complicated as courting cowboys and dudes.

Aunts and Butterflies

The beautiful blonde butterfly
takes flight, careens between cars,
heading straight for the street
where a sedan is speeding.
A monarch, orange and black
wings flapping, I fly
to the windshield.
Tires squeal to a stop.

Aunt Sharon saved your life,
her mother reminds her as we eat
turkey, dressing and cranberry
sauce until I move to California.
The whole family is here, says
her grandmother at Thanksgiving.

My little butterfly shakes her
blonde head. *No, Aunt Sharon*
isn't here. Her mother explains
I'm not blood, just a loving friend.
Everybody should have an
Aunt Sharon, she says.

Sunglasses, Bling and Lunch

Her dark hair flying
and her brown eyes
flashing, she is first
down the driveway
followed by her blonde
blue-eyed siblings.

She snatches my sun
glasses off my face,
my beads and baubles
off my neck and wrists
and wears them as I regal
her family with stories about
interviewing movie stars
on Hollywood Boulevard.

As we sleep over in her room,
she tries on my clothes
bought in Beverly Hills boutiques
and the next day we go to
Woolworth's to find her a bracelet,
necklace, sunglasses and a jump
suit like mine before we
eat roast beef sandwiches
at the counter on swivel stools.

One day when I visit, she holds
a figurine of a Siamese cat
in her small hand. *For you.*

When she gives birth to her
only daughter, she tells her
mother to call me and I smile
like a grandmother hearing
the sound of her first grandchild.

Big Heart

She has rheumatic fever,
her mother, my best friend,
tells me on the telephone,
as her eight-year-old daughter,
the baby of four children,
shrinks under hospital sheets
pale as oatmeal in milk
while her heart grows
to four times its size.

She'll never be able to finish
school or have a job or children,
say doctors which she defies,
struggling through school
getting her GED, emptying
bed pans and giving birth
to a healthy baby daughter.

She'll never be able to participate
in sports or any physical activities,
the doctors say as she walks
along the rim of the Grand Canyon,
climbs the Rocky Mountains
to watch her daughter ski
at the high school meet in Denver
and collects heart shaped rocks
in the Teton Mountains
for her family and friends.

She won't live past twenty without
open heart surgery, the doctors say.
But her big heart is still ticking
as her kidneys and liver fail her.
Mom, I'm fine. Don't worry, she says
the night before at forty-two she dies
as I sleep in my Arizona home
unaware the child who calls me
Aunt Sharon is leaving earth.

The Choice

He has no choice when his mother
dies giving him life with his father's
name sealed on her blue lips.

He has no choice when his adopted
mother chooses him and sits
with him during sickness and nightmares.

Walks him to school, makes him peanut
butter sandwiches, kisses his bruises
and laughs at his silly jokes.

But when he is ten he is asked
to make a choice at the Rose
Ceremony on Mother's Day.

White if your mother is dead.
Red if she is alive. The only mother
he has known is sitting stiff

on a folding chair and he knows
she wants to jump up and say,
It's okay if you choose her.

And he knows his birthmother
who is watching over him
wouldn't mind if he chose red.

But it is his choice. With his right
hand he reaches for the red rose
and with the left hand he picks the white,

sticks them in his buttonholes
and marches off with the troop
to salute their mothers.

In the Sixties Before Seat Belts and Dr. Phil

That's my school, he says pointing
to a sprawled out building where
children run and play on the grounds.

You're a liar, his teenage mother trills
from the front seat. *What a dummy.*
Your school is in Manhattan Beach.

It looks like your school, doesn't it?
I tell the toddler sitting between us
in the back seat of the Pontiac.

You are blind, Blondie. See the sign:
Santa Monica City Limits, my then
mother-in-law says with a smirk.

Hatred of the male child, her son
says as we build sandcastles
with our nephew while they shop.

They don't like me, the curly haired
cherub says as he plows his fist
into the twin towers and they collapse.

I like you both, I say and lift my
nephew in the air as his uncle
tackles me and we fall laughing.

I want to live with you, he begs
and my heart sinks like the sand
as he stands in the doorway crying.

I wonder if we had just turned around
if we could have prevented the disaster
that destroyed all of our lives.

She Too

Bill Cosby loves me, she says
at eighteen as she pulls panty
hose on her long lean limbs.
My agent always books me
for his parties as hostess.

I zipper her into a slinky
silk dress and she shuffles
all six feet of her out the door,
black hair bouncing down
her back to her buttocks.

Decades later, I wonder
how he removes her hose
and if he even bothers
to unzip her dress
as she lies on his bed
unconscious or confused
and how he piles her
in the cab and sends her home.

Distanced by divorce,
she never tells me or maybe
she never tells anyone
and maybe she never knows
or for some reason he spares her,
my innocent young sister-in-law.

Seven-Year-Old Twin Boys

In the San Miguel courtyard
in the late seventies, like salamanders,
they slink among the agaves
and red and blue bougainvillea
staring into mirror faces,
arms entwined like vines,
speaking sing songy
in a language of their own invention.

Their mother places three peas
on each of their plates with tofu
before she slips into the dress
she bought at the boutique
with her child support check
and runs off to the dinner party
to sip Chardonnay and dine
on oysters Rockefeller,
prime rib, roasted Brussel sprouts
and flaming cherry jubilee.

The twins crawl out the window
and sprawl on the roof
and sleep under a full moon,
their faces inches apart,
until they hear footsteps
on the cobblestone and climb back
through the window and slip under
cool cotton sheets and listen

to their mother moaning
in her bed with her professor.

She sits in the sun in her bikini
and when her boys throw arms
around her neck, she removes
them as if they are cobras
choking her, but when the tall
Swede from her sculpture
class walks towards her, she
lassos him with her rope arms.

One night a portly man shows
up at her door begging her
for another chance and she shoves
two suitcases and the twins at him
and the man disappears through the gate
with the twins tripping behind him
locked onto each other, not looking back.

I'm a terrible mother, she says. *I will*
never see my boys again. I sent them
to Florida with their father. But within
a week, the twins are back hip to hip,
face to face, dancing, singing, sleeping
on the roof while she hugs, kisses
and runs off to the Chinese Dragon
with the painter from Philadelphia.

The Girl with Three Mothers

When I see the four-year-old girl's
face peaked as a prune, hear her sniveling
and whining like the runt of the litter
as she sits on a pillow plunking
away on the Royal typewriter
like it's a grand piano, I figure
I can make her happy like the twins
I pick up from school and the eight-
year-old boy whose father left his
mother and him homeless. We all camp
on the couch and the spare bedroom
and the porch after I return to Escondido
from Mexico hunting for the perfect job.

But the little girl throws tantrums
and insists on sitting in her grandmother's
lap like a kangaroo baby in its mothers
pouch. I don't tell her that isn't her real grandma
but then that's not my real mother either,
although she thinks of me that way
giving me clothes that don't fit her anymore
and fixing me lunch as I run off to
Montgomery Wards to sell clothes
with her daughter-in-law.

Her biological mother died. Accident,
I think, my second mother says. It isn't until
I get the PR job and am moving to Encinitas
that the little girl starts cuddling up to me.

The only time I see her laughing and smiling
is when we sleep in a tent, eat hot dogs
and smores scorched in a campfire
at the Sierra Club campout for disadvantaged
children and when we eat pizza and chocolates
forbidden by her parents who are vegetarians.
at my table in my new house. When she is forty
and her grandmother is gone, we hike together.

She is still stunted and doesn't smile but she
is calm and quiet and talks as if we are strangers.
I had three mothers, she says showing me
photos of her birth mother and her father's
second and third wives. She's a psychiatrist,
never married and childless, she tells me.

I ask if she remembers camping with me
and having sleepovers at my beach house.
Did I beg you for sweets? I wasn't allowed sugar.
She pauses. *Do you know why my mother killed
herself right after I was born? Was I bad?*

Mute and Meek in the Seventies

In camouflage and a buzz cut,
the small soldier smashes
the piñata with his toy rifle
at his sixth birthday party
as the newspaper photographer
snaps his shutter and I take
notes for the story for the weekly
down the block in Encinitas.

After his mother goes back
to her shift at McDonalds
and the children leave in cars,
I return from work to find,
a woman and two children
sitting on the steps of the house.
Visiting from Los Angeles,
she says disappearing into the house
while her mute and meek children
and I mold sand monkeys
in the box between our two houses.

On the weekend a muffler pops
like gunfire and a muscular man
jumps off a motorcycle and the kids
scatter off the sidewalk and hide
behind the house. I hear shouting,
slapping and crying until Monday
when he roars off. The kids are mute

while cold water runs over their hands
and I put cool wash clothes on bruised
bodies. I knock. Their mother doesn't
answer the door so I feed them peanut
butter and jelly sandwiches and milk.

One day after work, I put the children
in my Chevrolet and drive to the beach.
I turn around halfway down
the steep hill when the children
scream and shake in terror.
Their mother has gone to Los Angeles,
my neighbor tells me a week later.
She gives permission for the children
to go into my house and her son follows.

He turns off the faucets when the children
soak their hands and cuts the crust
as I make peanut butter sandwiches.
When the five-year-old boy says he wants
crust on his bread, soldier boy punches him
in the groin and when he gasps for breath,
his sister cries and I say, *NO. We do not hit
in this house.* Stone faced he marches out
the door. I am consoling the two children
when my neighbor sticks her head in the door
and smiling stiffly summons the terrified children.
That's the last time I see any of them. When
I return from my camping trip the house
is empty and a plastic pail rolls in the courtyard.

Dumpster Diving for Comic Books

The banging and clanging
in the alley behind the bookstore
escalates as the garbage truck empties
the dumpster, then car tires squeal
and speed away. Before I empty
my waste basket, I look down
and see hundreds of comic
books lying at the bottom
of the huge dumpster like
shiny pearls in the ocean.
Comic books are in demand
but no one would part with them.

I hear children's voices
and guarding my bounty, I call
out to them and a boy about eight
and two girls approximately six
and four run towards me.
I promise them free books if they
help me retrieve the comic books.

I instruct the boy to get a chair
from the bookstore and lift his baby
sister and she climbs into the dumpster
and like a factory assembly line
the youngest hands the comics
to her sister and brother and they carry
them to the back room and pile them
on the windowsill as I protect

the precious child from neighbors
throwing runny egg yolks
and rotten tomatoes on her freshly
shampooed head and clean clothes.

I also pray their great grandmother
doesn't come racing out of the gate
like a greyhound and call the cops
and have me arrested for child abuse.
When our mission is accomplished
and the children and comic books
are safely inside the store, I call
my 75-year-old neighbor and ask
if her grandkids can help me in the store.

Ten years later, the boy now a tall teen
walks in the bookstore and shows me
his two Batman comic books still looking
brand new and says he wouldn't trade
them and offers me a tiny figurine of a cat
and Bible. *I remember how you liked*
cats and your mother was a saint. He recalls
the taste of the curly fries and pepperoni
pizza she served them for lunch. *We loved*
helping you clean the shelves and box
the books. No one was ever that kind
to us before except our grandmother.

You must miss her, I say. *I didn't even*
know she was sick until the funeral, he says.
I remember the Buick knocking Margaret
on her back in the supermarket parking lot,
the surgeon fileting her belly like a fisherman,

finding her full of cancer and closing her up
and her moving in with a granddaughter.
He hugs me goodbye and hops on his bike
and disappears just like his grandmother.

Toads and Petroglyphs

Get up lady, the five-year-old says
as he x-rays me with dark eyes
and rips the sheet off my body.
Groggy on codeine and penicillin
after a yanked molar, I blink.

You're mean lady, he says
when I snatch the Coca-Cola
and Hershey bar from him
and fix him a glass of milk
and bowl of granola for breakfast.

Catch me if you can, he shrieks
as he runs out the door of the RV
and up the hill behind the house site
where his father and my husband
carry logs and place them on the ceiling.

I give chase and heart valve flopping,
lose my balance, but he pops out
from behind an Ironwood.
Hanging onto the tree, he grabs
my hand and steadies me.

You're pretty cool lady, he says
as we see Sonoran toads swimming
and serenading us in the Indian Baths.
We walk up to the rocks and he jumps
with joy as he views sketches

of his Native American ancestors.

Can you spare a dollar lady, he says
at twenty-years-old as he stands
on a street corner, arms and neck
tattooed like the petroglyphs,
his dark hair dirty and disheveled.
His eyes muddy as his jeans,
he sucks on an empty Coors bottle
he picks up from the gutter.

Do you remember me? I want to ask
but the woman who points him out
keeps on driving, reminding me
that he was raised on the streets
by drunks and druggies and that's
all he knows. But the mother in me
still remembers the five-year-old boy
who thought toads and I were cool
and she wants to take him home.

The Barber's Granddaughter

I was born in prison, says
the five-year-old in braids
and a pink Miss Piggy t-shirt
dangling pudgy legs as she colors
a clown and her gray grandfather
whispers, *Her mother is a murderer,*
while snipping my husband's hair.

Daddy's here, she says as a horn honks,
jumps up and holds out her hand.
I need a new Barbie. He empties
his tip jar of dollar bills and she tucks
them in both pockets and runs out the door.
I hope my son doesn't spend it on heroin,
the barber says, sharpening his blade.

Daddy died in a car wreck, she says
as she turns six and her grandmother
drops her off. *Late for the cardiologist*
appointment, the white-haired woman
mutters as she kisses the chubby cheek.
My wife just had open heart surgery,
the barber says as his granddaughter
pats his Santa belly and laughs.

Grandma died of a broken heart,
she says as she sweeps up the hair
around my husband's feet. *My third*
grade teacher gave me straight A's.

The barber hobbles on a walker.
I've got to hang on for her. He slurs
out of the crooked side of his face.
Her mama got Life Without Parole.

Teen Twin Invasion

Their mother catches Covid
after the cruise to Cancun
and their father is being
dispatched on a business
trip to Berlin so he puts
the twins on the Red Eye
from San Francisco
to Portland where their uncle
picks them up and drives
them to their grandparent's
townhouse in the suburbs.

When their fourteen-year-old
twin grandson and granddaughter
wake them with waffles
smothered in strawberry syrup
and coffee with sugar and cream,
Grandpa clutches his heart
and Grandma almost dislocates
a hip, but in the afternoon
when she watches the girl,
blonde and violet eyed like
her mother, cradling the head
of her son's baby boy,
as he drinks water from a bottle,

and her twin brother, dark eyes
like his Jewish father, tinkering
with a Tonka truck for his toddler
cousin, she smiles at the grandbabies
she never thought she would have.
The embryos planted in wombs.
The miracles she and her soulmate
now in their eighties had wished
for when they said their vows
sixty years ago in the chapel
on the Las Vegas Strip
where she paid for dinner
by winning $50 in the slots.

Doppelganger Daughter

When the tall lanky millennium
who just bought land up the road
tells me his girlfriend looks just
like me and has my mannerisms,
I am skeptical but curious.

But when the twenty-something
schoolteacher walks through
the door with a pixie cut, saucer
eyes dominating elfin face,
giggling, fingers fluttering,
I feel like I am in a time capsule,
watching my twenty-something self.

You look just like Goldie Hawn,
I say like everyone said to me
when I was her age. Of course,
she has no idea who I am talking
about. She points to my younger
photos plastering the wall.
Is that Goldie Hawn? she asks.

When all the neighbors file in
with their casserole dishes
and salads, they tell her:
You look just like your mom.
If I doubt she exists, all I do
is look at the wall and there
we stand, two golden goddesses
with identical cheekbones and smiles.

Black Eyed Susan

After the Garden of Eden prophet dies,
two men in suits carry her out
of the commune down to the road,
her long goldilocks waving in the wind.
yellow dress dragging in the dirt,
dark eyes darting like a rabbit
as they deposit her outside the gate
and she yanks on the chains, *Let me*
back in, she calls, *I can't breathe.*

The prophet taught us to stay inside,
that the air outside was poison gas,
she takes a deep breath of the ocean
air as we walk along the beach
near the Encinitas weekly newspaper
where she writes headlines instead
of making them and I write stories
a decade after the scandal broke.

.

In pantyhose and skirt to her knees,
her hair its natural brown, Jeanette,
her birth name, recalls the day
she meets the prophet and her life changes.
His hypnotic green eyes stared
right into my soul, and she boards
his Volkswagen bus for Laramie
right after graduation from Colorado State.

We were his children, she says. *I still miss*
hm telling me what to do and what to wear.
He names female followers after flowers.
They weren't allowed to use birth names.
I was his favorite, she says, which is why
his widow had her cast out. The cult leaves
Escondido for Des Moines leaving her behind.
I would have done anything for him, she says.

Two decades later, I wonder if she
would have ingested a Euthanasia cocktail,
lie down on her bunk and waited
for a spaceship to beam her up
to Heaven in the Rancho Santa Fe
mansion like the thirty-eight followers
of another prophet with hypnotic eyes.

The Mamas

Best Mom in the World

She dives like a swan in the blue
sky in her satin wedding gown
as her groom in black and white
tuxedo and shirt lifts her above
his head. *Won't we make beautiful
babies?* she asks fingering the photo.

But you hate children. I remember
when we were rival reporters
attending parties on the weekend
and I was upstairs reading bedtime
stories to the children of the hosts
while she was hunting for Mr. Right.

After she is promoted as editor
of the social page and meets
the handsome architect
and trust fund baby, she flashes
a two carat diamond ring.
We can afford a houseful of kids.

*We'll just hire someone else
to take care of them. And I'm
not going to ruin my firm boobs
and flat stomach so we'll pay
a surrogate to go through
morning sickness and labor pains.*

I am surprised when years later
while visiting the San Diego Republic,

I spot her sitting in the break room
drinking coffee out of a mug, engraved:
Best Mom in the World, as she tells
me she is quitting to be a full time mom.

I gave two weeks notice today. I joined
the gym and signed up for Zumba, Yoga,
Pilates and Aerobics. Moms must be fit.
When I arrive for dinner at her four-story
home on the hill overlooking La Jolla
beach, a middle-aged woman answers the door.

Madame is soaking in the bubble bath
before she dresses for dinner. She escorts
me into the family room where a young
fit brunette in a ponytail and jogging suit
is putting shoes on the toddler. Four
blond boys greet me with a curtsy and a smile.

I play scrabble with the six- and eight-year-olds
while bouncing the toddler on my knee
as the four-year-old stares with saucer eyes.
Whiskey, vodka or rum? the tall suit
says as he sticks his head in the room.
Just a glass of ice water will be fine.

The kitchen door swings open and a man
in a chef's apron and hat exits with my water
as the scent of meatloaf and mushrooms
mixes with musk and lavender on her skin
as madame waltzes down the stairs
in stiletto heels and turquoise gown.

We're going to the country club, she announces,
handing me a slinky red dress that fits like a stocking.
I told you not to touch Mommy. It's adult time,
she says as the nannies whisk away the boys.
Isn't she the best mom? asks her husband
as we get into the Maserati and drive away.

Soap Opera Mamas

You're sure you want me to bring him over?
He's crawling and putting everything in his mouth.
I tell her it's fine. I'll vacuum and shampoo
the carpet. She puts him down on the floor
and we start watching *All My Children*
and spot him by the bed stuffing a dust bunny
in his mouth. I apologize but she says
he can find dirt anywhere. He smells
of Johnson's & Johnson's baby powder and milk
as he sleeps in my arms. We discuss plots
for soap operas we are going to write
together when we get to Hollywood.

Then the talk turns to my new boyfriend
with a daughter named Melba. She laughs.
Melba Toast? I tell her he's a great guy,
another reporter and we talk for hours.
but he insists his twenty-one-year-old
daughter go everywhere we go. He says
he is studying to be a lawyer so he never
has to retire. When I die, she'll have
to get herself a sugar daddy, he tells me.
She stares spellbound eating every word.

Melba works at Ace's Hardware but she
talks baby talk and lives in the same
bedroom she lived in before her father
kicked her alcoholic mother to the curb.
Why ever leave home when she gets free

room and board? He even buys her cigarettes.
My soap opera groupie asks me what Mona
would say as the baby awakens and they go.

I tell my boyfriend it's Melba or me
and he chooses her and I move to Idaho.
My friend calls and says she's divorced
and lost her house because her husband
spent all their savings on sugar he thought
was cocaine. *He was just going to make*
a killing so I wouldn't have to work.
We could have both gone to prison
and the baby would have gone into foster care.
Who needs to write soap operas, w*e* decide
when we're both living in one.

Baby Makers

The one-year-old's breathing
is like static on the radio.
We can hear it through the walls.
When I knock on their door,
she insists her baby is not sick.
Even if he was, she has no car.
I offer to drive them to the clinic
and she reluctantly agrees
while his two-year-old brother
stays with my eighty-year-old mother.

In the cubicle, she places him
on his back and he chokes on phlegm.
I pick him up and put a diaper
on my shoulder and pat him
on the back. When the doctor
comes in, she takes him from me
and puts him back on his back.

Pick that baby up, the doctor barks.
He listens to the chest and back
and prescribes antibiotics. I offer
to pick up the prescription
on our way home but she says
when we get home she will call
friends to take her to pick
up the prescription.

She plops the baby in my mother's
lap and I find the prescription
and her Medicaid card on the counter
after she rides off with her friends.
The pharmacist at the corner drug store
where I fill my mother's prescriptions
finally hands me the medicine
when I explain we are babysitting the boy.

When the new baby comes, his cries
penetrate the walls at 5 am. *Shut up!*
a male voice yells. *We are sleeping.*
She tells me her husband is home on leave
to help her with the new baby.
I tell a former social worker as she hunts
for romance novels. *Don't bother to call*
CPS. He'll probably kill the poor baby
and you too. You can't fix stupid.

He is deployed to the Middle East
and she moves in with her mother-in-law.
Months later, I spot the kids in Albertson's
crammed in a shopping cart
pushed by a white-haired lady
who looks like she never sleeps. I hear
her on the cell phone complaining
about being stuck with her grandkids
since her son was in military prison
overseas and her daughter-in-law ran
off with another guy to California.
The kids look happy and healthy.
And that's all I care about.

The Woman With Fifteen Children

Gray hair in a bun, age spots
and wrinkles on her square face,
she drags her sagging body
to the chair where she skims
through the Harlequin romances
to make sure they don't have
any dirty stuff, she says.

Each time she pays, she tells me
this will be the last time I will see her
because her daughter is coming
from California to take her to live
with her. Summer turns to fall
and fall to winter and then to spring
and she tells me the same story.

After five years, she stops mentioning
her daughter and so I ask about her.
Which one? she says. *I have fifteen*
children. I gasp. *Where do they live?*
I ask. *I don't know*, she says.

She sits on a bench in the park
reading a Harlequin and eating an apple
as I run on the trail on a Sunday.
When I approach her she tosses
the book and apple in her cart and flees.

The next time she enters the bookstore
she is shivering in the cold temperatures
in her thin jacket and stockings and sandals
and coughing and sneezing all over the books.

I ask again about her children and she rattles
off first names and describes them as toddlers
or pre-school age and I wonder if these children
were taken from her or if they exist only in her mind.

Her death notice appears in the newspaper
the same day as my mother's. It says she died
in her sleep and lists no survivors.

Mother Knows Best

Red Skeleton's daughter.
is my husband's secretary,
Pauline tells her parents when
they fly into LA from Omaha.
Valentina? Let me meet her.
I'd recognize her on sight,
says her mother as her father
picks up the suitcases.

She is off for the weekend,
Pauline's husband says, squirming
like a worm. *Do you know*
the family? he asks.
Very well, her mother says,
I saw Red every week on TV
and I read in the movie magazines
about her brother's death
from Leukemia and her mother's
heart attack. I'd love to hug her
and tell her how sorry I am.

He smiles and says he will arrange
it as he drives to Santa Monica.
A woman calls the house and asks
for Pauline's husband. *Valentina?*
her mother asks and gets a dial tone.
Couldn't have been her she's
attending a function
with her father in Hollywood,

Pauline's husband says as he steps
out to smoke a Lucky Strike.
I recognized Valentina's voice,
her mother insists. Pauline laughs.

On the news, the red haired
comedian wins an award.
Valentina is nowhere
to be seen and neither
is Pauline's husband. *I know*
they are having an affair.
her mother says. *Nonsense*,
Pauline says as she keeps
his plate warm all night..

.

I told you so, her mother says
as Pauline types *adultery*
on the divorce papers.
By the way, Valentina's
mother shot herself to death.
I bet Valentina is off
somewhere with your husband.

Pauline turns on the TV and Valentina
and Red are dodging the paparazzi.
and her husband is nowhere to be seen.
I bet he is in a motel waiting for Valentina,
her mother says. *Good Riddance*,
Pauline says as she signs the papers.

Blood Mother

The boy blows bubbles in the bath
as I shampoo the mashed bananas
out of his blond curls and squirms
as I wrap him in a towel, toddles
and wobbles to the door crying *Mama*
when my friend rings the doorbell.

The judge gave his father weekend
visitation although he threatened
to drown him if I didn't come back.

I look into eyes as blue as the sky
as his lips smack me on the cheek
and he waves goodbye as he walks
bow legged across the grass to the condo
holding his mother's hand and disappears
into the doorway after his mother smothers
him with kisses and hugs and tears.
He is still in his Dodger cap and jacket
when he is found floating face down
in the river two days after he goes missing.

Breaking News the brunette anchor
says as she stands in front of yellow tape
and the camera pans to my friend
falling to her knees screaming, *He killed*
my baby. And the boy's father saying,
It was an accident. He fell out of the boat.
I grab my keys and drive to the dock.

Strangulation. No water in lungs.
Homicide, the coroner says.
while photos of the blue-eyed boy
with the trusting face are shown
and his mother sobs as the sheriff
announces the arrest of the boy's
father, the leather jacket over his face,
the hands that killed his own blood
behind his back, wrists in handcuffs.
in his perp walk for the TV cameras.

We finally got justice for my son,
the woman with wrinkles and gray
hair says decades later on the internet
as I watch from my Arizona home.
My baby's murderer, his father
was executed while I watched.
Voice breaking, she holds a photo
of her blue-eyed smiling angel.
My son's blood is on the robe
of the judge who sent him to his death.
She should have gotten the needle too.

The Perfect Mother

With auburn curls bouncing
against her apple cheeks,
washboard abs and legs
like a thoroughbred,
she jogs through
the neighborhood in San
Diego pushing her toddler
in the stroller or bicycles
pulling him in a wagon.

Mother and son plant tulips
and gladiolas and she pushes
him in the swing and dips
her toes in his wading pool
as he splashes, their laughter
echoing in the breeze even
as her belly balloons until
it pops and she gasps
and drives herself to the hospital
after strapping her son in his car
seat in the back of her SUV.

She returns carrying a red faced
baby in a pink blanket as the boy
skips ahead. A few weeks later,
I am nursing a head cold when I
see the boy without his mother
dragging a laundry basket

across my lawn and then tapping
on my window like a woodpecker.

I put on my bathrobe and open
the door and walk out and hear
a mewing coming from the basket
and see a baby flailing her arms
and legs and pick her up. She smells
like urine and sour milk. He disappears
through my open door before I can
return him to his mother. A steak knife
falls out oi his pocket. *What's this?*
I ask as he munches on an apple.

Mommy gave it to me. She told me
to kill the baby. I don't know how.
Maybe you could do it, he says.
Just then I hear sirens and police
cars pull up in her driveway. I fear
she's called them because she's
realized her children were missing
and I will be arrested for kidnapping.
Postpartum Depression, says the man
the boy calls *Daddy. I always told him*
to go to the neighbors if he needed help.

The Baby Mama From Hell

Rape, she cries when her mother
catches her boyfriend leaving
her bedroom at daybreak
and hauls her down to the police
station and presses charges.

As the nurse examines her,
she texts her boyfriend. *I lied*
and said you raped me
because I am two weeks
pregnant and mom will kick
me out for having sex.

He shows the text to the two armed
policemen waiting in the school hallway
when the Algebra teacher tells him
he has visitors. No charges are filed.

We will raise the baby, the boy's
family says and she says: *Goodie.*
Can I move in too? His mother says:
No and he asks for his promise ring back.
She marches down to the police station
to get him put in prison and on the Sex
Offenders List. *See if you can get*
another girlfriend now, she texts.

There is no evidence of a rape,
the policeman tells her.
We can charge you for filing

a false police report and shows her
the text. She denies sending it.
The cops are crooked, she texts.

I don't care if they are both
sixteen, you can't adopt a baby
out without the father's consent,
five adoption lawyers tell her
mother. She keeps the baby,
leaves the father's name
off the birth certificate, files
for child support but refuses
to allow him to see the baby.
I know my rights, she says.

For four years, her mother raises
the baby while she spends her child
support money on perfume, jewelry
and tight jeans and sexy tops
and bounces like a beach ball
from bed to bed looking for a new baby daddy
until the birth father files for custody.

*The judge is allowing my rapist to see
my child*, she tells her housemates,
neighbors, mechanic and hairdresser.
Outrageous, they say. The Baby Daddy
turns up missing after his last visit.
Why is his truck in your driveway?
the cops ask. *He drove off with a blonde
in a red sportscar,* she says smiling sweetly
as the cops stare at the mound of dirt
under the maple tree behind the house.

His Mother

watches him from across
the room with wide eyes
as steady as a movie camera,

flat ears tuning in to a frequency
only a mother can hear,
listening for pending danger:

a cough, uneven breath,
the sound of glass breaking
or strange footsteps on the stairs,

lips parted as if the right words
lie frozen on the tip of her tongue
like the icicles on the porch.

Although she watches his wardrobe
change as he stretches from
twenty inches to six foot three,

his mother always wears her red
silk dress with white pearls and
two-inch-high platform heels,

and her hands, which remain by her side
and out of the sun and soapy water, remain
as soft as when she held him that one time.

Lost

The little boy who sang
off key in the church choir,
caught house spiders in jars
and released them into the grass,

planted her a rose bush
for Mother's Day
and mowed grandma's lawn
when she broke her hip.

She can't find him
in the mugshot
on the front page
of the newspaper,

in the defendant
in the orange jumpsuit
who hobbles in shackles
across the courtroom,

or the stranger
who stares at her
through the glass
with dead eyes.

He is gone,
but not the love for him
she wears like a coat
when she steps into the night.

Mistake

He is twelve and you are slathering
barbecue sauce on chicken wings
when a policeman who bowls
on your league informs you
your son is being held at the police station
for stealing a pack of gum
from the corner convenience store.

You say it has to be a mistake.
Your son has just earned
his Boy Scout badge for honesty.
You pay for the gum.
The store owner,
a friend from high school,
agrees to drop the charges.

He is fifteen and you are pulled
out of a deep sleep by a ringing
as shrill as a fire alarm.
The policeman says your son is in handcuffs
after being caught flying high
in a stolen car with the new friends
he met a school.

You say it has to be a mistake.
You saw his bare feet sticking
out under the comforter on his bed
just a few hours ago.
You pay the lawyer from the family

vacation fund and your son gets probation
and a new set of friends.

He is eighteen and you just arrived
home from picking up
his cap and gown when
the phone rings and you hear
a computer like voice say:
This is The Correction Facility.
Will you accept a collect call from:

You tell yourself it has to be a mistake
as you hear his voice breaking and swallow
every maple syrupy lie he spoon feeds you
about being framed for bank robbery.
You take out a loan to hire the best lawyer in town
and put up the house to bail him out
in time for the graduation ceremony.

He is twenty-one and you are living with the in laws
and feeding your younger children peanut butter after
he flies south like the migrating geese. Voicemail picks
up the calls as you scurry from your day job to your
night job. You scan the messages hoping to hear his voice
and sometimes at night you wake up believing you hear
him breathing down the hall and it is all a mistake.

In Buddy's Bar and Grill

Long neck ice cold beer
never broke my heart,
the corn-fed farm boy
mimics Luke Coombs
in the microphone,
while the brandy cheeked
barmaid whisks away
empty Corona bottles
in the crowded corner
where the tattooed blonde
and the big biceped bartender
down Jack Daniels shots
as her tow-headed toddler
sits strapped in a car seat
in the back seat of the Buick
in the sizzling summer sun.

Facebook Mom

My Lil' Man she calls her dimpled
darling in disposable diapers,
pacifier stuffed in his mouth
like a pig roasting on a spit.

He watches from his baby seat
as his mother shows off white
teeth, cleavage and bare legs
in the selfies she posts daily.

My Lil' Man loves his mama,
she tells her 155 friends.
You are a good Mom,
her friends respond.

.

He is lucky to have you,
as her Lil Man's bald head falls
face down in spit up on his chest.
like a passed out drunk.

Suburban Stay at Home Mom

She squints as sunshine slants
and her five-year-old sails
through the room, drags
her out of bed and up the hill,
her bad breath blowing
in the air, hands trembling.
Her nightgown is plastered
to her blossoming bosom
and baby bump. *The flu,*
she explains. Last week
it was *Covid.* Her son's
teacher doesn't buy it,
gives her the same
disapproving evil eye
as her baby daddy,
his family, hers and her pastor
who preaches about sinners
like her, but all she wants
is to crawl under the covers
with her lover, Jim Beam.

We Had a Love Child, Bobby Says

I heard it on the grapevine,
you two dated back in Montana
in your teens, the barmaid blubbers
as she hands me an iced tea
and him a draft. The drunks
around the table are all ears.

She came into the Dairy Queen
and I sold her a curly top cone
and we fell head over heels.
His blue eyes sparkle
over his bushy white beard.
Heads swivel and eyes stare
as I blush like the Bougainvillea's
crawling up the patio wall.

Cut your BS, my husband says.
You never met my wife until
we retired in Arizona. He hands
the beer back to the barmaid
and his bandmate says: *She dumped*
me for the basketball star who
married my other girlfriend,
and the crowd murmurs, *Right Bobby.*
as he grabs his guitar and sings,
Your Cheating Heart directly to me.

Roadie

She looks like a Barbie Doll
with her painted face and nails,
synthetic breasts rising

under her pink T-shirt,
long lean legs in skinny jeans,
small feet in slingback stiletto sandals.

Under a red Cardinals Baseball cap,
her hair flows to her shoulders,
once golden, now silver

as the Navajo bracelets that jangle
on both wrists as she carries
the electric guitar and microphone

for the Kenny Rogers lookalike,
she has followed cross country
for a quarter of a century.

Her face is a roadmap of where
they've been since she left
her children behind with their father

in the trailer park eating pizza
and drinking coca cola
and watching a Braves game,

but the past is about to catch up
as their adult faces shine
in the audience like a neon sign.

Barfly

She smiles in a pretty face,
lifted and botoxed,
until all the wrinkles

are as smooth as the sheets
where she entertains
the men she meets in the saloon

as she sips sugared daiquiris
and salted margaritas
and buzzes through the crowd,

swaying on mechanical hips
and knees on the dance floor,
a head resting on breast implants

and lands at midnight in the lap,
of a man, young, old, married
or not, she doesn't care

as long as he leaves before
the harsh daylight reveals her turkey
neck and senior citizen skin.

Talk Me Off the Ledge, she says

with that wry laugh. *I've had a bad MS*
day and I've got cysts in my breasts.
What if the cancer comes back?
What if I don't live to be sixty-four?

Everything will be fine. I'm psychic
remember? She calls back. *My mammogram*
was clear. I just published my eighth book
and I've got four cruises booked this year.

Back from the Caribbean islands,
she gets shingles on her neck
and ear. The doctor wants her
to take another mammogram.

But she's going to the Bahamas
in March, France in April
and the Panama Canal in November.
Stay in bed, you're dead, she says.

Sally is missing, she says on her cell.
My little girl went out last night
and never came home. Her brother
went looking for her and now he's gone.

She says she and the neighbors
were searching all night. *Someone*
spotted a coyote near our house.
Those Siamese were my babies.

Body or Baby?

She is groggy but the Mexican
woman who can't speak English
in the Tijuana clinic
wipes the blood gushing like
a geyser, shoves a pad between
her legs and pushes her out
the door and stuffs her in a cab
and the driver drops her off
in the alley of the cheap motel.

The next day she buys drugs
on the corner to ease the pain
and hobbles to the corner stop
and boards the bus to El Cajon.
After all the passengers file out
the bus driver finds her passed
out with a weak pulse as blood
pools around her swollen feet.

The paramedics pronounce her dead.
Botched abortion, the authorities
tell her husband standing in the doorway,
grease on his hands and uniform
as three small children cry,
When's mommy coming home daddy?

The husband tells the press:
I didn't know she was pregnant.
I thought she was visiting her mother

and sister in Los Angeles,
as protesters march carrying signs:
Stop killing babies. Her body,
Her choice. Now she has neither,
I think in the sixties before Roe
and think the same thing now
as I read about Roe being overturned.

Surrogate Daughter

Taboada Hot Springs, Mexico 1976

Mesmerizing as a mirage,
slick as a seal, he slides
into the water beside me

where I soak up to my neck
in whirling water hot
as a Jalapeno pepper.

This dark-eyed Don Juan
whispers words in Spanish
soft and succulent as Sandia.

I imagine he is reciting:
Love me tender, love me
sweet, never let me go.

But my interpreter
tells me: *He says you look*
just like his sister-in-law.

You're joking. I laugh
as my Romeo shouts
Look who's here

and two women speaking
rapidly in Spanish run
toward me shrieking *Rosa.*

They stop short and shake
their heads as they stare at me.
She looks just like her, doesn't she?

They nod and the older woman
coaxes me out of the hot water
and guides me up the stairs

to her room where she shows me
photos of a pretty woman my age
with dark hair and brown eyes like mine.

I can't see the resemblance.
But I sit on the bed with this woman
who speaks a different language,

and I put my head on her square shoulder
and let her brush my hair and plant
kisses on my cheek and call me Rosa over and over

because I know what it's like to love and lose children
and then find them again only to have them slip
out of your reach and fly away like sparrows.

www.ingramcontent.com/pod-product-compliance
Lightning Source LLC
Chambersburg PA
CBHW050024170726
48282CB00025B/539
* 9 7 8 9 3 9 0 6 0 1 9 4 3 *